SURVIVING TERROR

TRUE TEEN STORIES FROM AROUND THE WORLD

True Teen Stories from

NIGERIA

Surviving Boko Haram

Kristin Thiel

Cavendish Square

New York

Published in 2019 by Cavendish Square Publishing, LLC
243 5th Avenue, Suite 136, New York, NY 10016

Cataloging-in-Publication Data

Names: Thiel, Kristin.
Title: True teen stories from Nigeria: surviving Boko Haram / Kristin Thiel.
Description: New York : Cavendish Square, 2019. | Series: True teen
stories from around the world | Includes glossary and index.
Identifiers: ISBN 9781502635556 (pbk.) | ISBN 9781502635532
(library bound) | ISBN 9781502635549 (ebook)
Subjects: LCSH: Boko Haram. | Terrorist organizations--Nigeria. | Terrorism--Nigeria-
-Religious aspects--Islam. | Islamic fundamentalism--Nigeria. | Teenagers--Nigeria.
Classification: LCC HV6433.N62 T54 2019 | DDC 363.32509669--dc23

Editorial Director: David McNamara
Editor: Caitlyn Miller
Copy Editor: Rebecca Rohan
Associate Art Director: Alan Sliwinski
Production Coordinator: Karol Szymczuk
Photo Research: J8 Media

The photographs in this book are used by permission and through the courtesy of:
Cover Philip Ojisua/AFP/Getty Images; p. 4, 94 Stefan Heunis/AFP/Getty Images;
p. 7 Pavalena/Shutterstock.com; p. 8, 48 Pius Utomi Ekpei/AFP/Getty Images; p. 13
Staff Sgt. Christopher Klutts, U.S. Army/Wikimedia Commons/File:Flintlock 2017
marksmanship training in Niger 170301ABV528009.jpg/Public Domain; p. 21 Ivan
Kuzmin/Shutterstock.com; p. 25 Evening Standard/Getty Images; p. 28 Agence Opale/
Alamy Stock Photo; p. 38 Jossy Ola/AP Images; p. 47 Branco, courtesy Americans
for Limited Government; p. 55 Bryan Alexander/Wikimedia Commons/File:Nnedi
Okorafor (37108184821).jpg/CC BY 2.0; p. 56 Xinhua/Olawale Salau/Getty Images;
p. 59 Alexander Klein/AFP/Getty Images; p 65 Sunday Alamba/AP Images; p. 67
Florian Plaucheur/AFP/Getty Images; p. 80 Adekunle Ajayi/NurPhoto/Getty Images.

Printed in the United States of America

CONTENTS

Due to Boko Haram's violence, this boy was forced to leave his home and move to a camp for internally displaced persons, or refugees who live within their home country.

CHAPTER ONE

NIGERIA, BOKO HARAM, AND DAILY LIFE IN A FASCINATING PART OF THE WORLD

Boko Haram is a terrorist organization causing destruction and adding to instability in Nigeria, a country in western Africa. Increasingly, Boko Haram's reach extends to neighboring countries, such as Cameroon. The organization's attacks are growing more violent, forcing more people to flee their homes without warning. Youth are coerced into becoming soldiers, kidnapped and held as hostages, and displaced from their schools and communities when Boko Haram militants destroy their towns. However, young people are standing up to Boko Haram and making positive changes in Nigeria and the world.

Nigeria and Boko Haram: Setting the Stage

Nigeria is a large, diverse country. Physically, it is bigger than Texas and features wet coastal areas and dry deserts. It is the most populous African country. Altogether, Nigerians speak hundreds of languages and come from 250 ethnic groups. Each group claims its own territory within the country.

Nigeria is wealthy in some ways: it is a major producer of oil and natural gas, it has the second largest economy in Africa, and the richest person in Africa is Nigerian. However, many of its citizens struggle every day to survive. Of Nigeria's 186 million citizens, 100 million live on less than $1 a day.

Boko Haram is both a product of Nigeria's uniqueness and a force working to destroy it. A Muslim cleric started the militant group in 2002. At first, a lot of people saw Boko Haram as a force for much-needed change in Nigeria. The government was corrupt, and people were divided by wealth and religion. (Since 1960, most people practice Islam or Christianity.) Boko Haram promised clarity and unity. However, the group's foundation is in damaging—and often false—religious claims. Over the years, it has relied on increasingly violent tactics to push its agenda and make others conform to it.

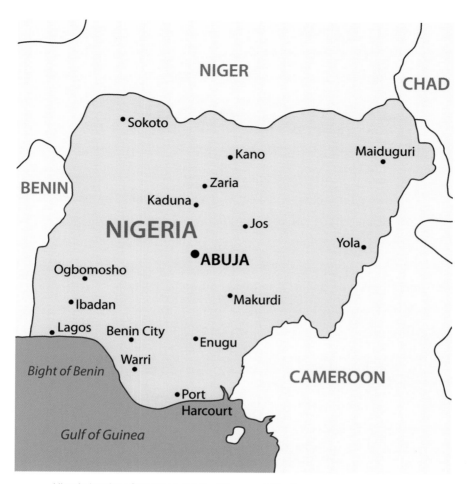

Nigeria borders Cameroon, Benin, Niger, and Chad.

Boko Haram has taken the lives of many young Nigerians. The United Nations estimated that the number of children used as human bombs quadrupled from 2016 to 2017. Fifty-six girls, most younger than fifteen, and twenty-seven boys were killed that year because the terrorist group

ABUBAKAR SHEKAU

Abubakar Shekau is the second leader of Boko Haram. He replaced the group's founder, Muhammed Yusuf, after Yusuf was killed in police custody in 2009. Though there are occasional rumors Shekau has been replaced as leader, as of 2018, he was believed to remain in control. Under Shekau's leadership, Boko Haram has become more violent than ever. The BBC has called him "part-theologian, part-gangster." In

A wanted poster for Abubakar Shekau offers a reward of about $320,000 (in American currency) for information on his whereabouts.

a video in which he admitted to kidnapping a large group of female students in 2014, he laughed as he said, "I will sell them in the market, by Allah. I will sell them off and marry them off."

Shekau's last name is the same as the name of the village in which he was born; the town of Shekau is in Nigeria's northeastern state of Yobe. No one knows exactly how old Boko Haram's leader is. Many estimates place his year of birth sometime in the 1970s. Few people, even members of Boko Haram, have seen him.

Shekau met Yusuf through a mutual friend, Mamman Nur. At the time, all three were students of theology, or religion. All three were also considered politically radical. They demonstrated this in their actions. Yusuf started Boko Haram, and Shekau took the leadership next. Nur was believed to have planned the 2011 bombing of the United Nations offices in Nigeria's capital, Abuja. When Yusuf died, Shekau married one of his wives. Shekau had four wives, until a raid killed his wife Mallama Fitdasi in 2017.

used them to carry bombs—and by detonating their bombs, the terrorist group killed many more people, some of them children. Boko Haram also lures young people to become their soldiers. Sometimes the militants promise a salary or a better life, and sometimes they threaten children and teens into joining. The United Nations estimated that Boko Haram recruited two thousand children in 2016. The group also abducts young people; one of the most well-known cases was the 2014 armed kidnapping of more than two hundred high school students, who would come to be known as the Chibok girls. An estimated one million children no longer have schools to attend because Boko Haram has destroyed their school buildings or because threats of violence have left school officials no choice but to cancel classes.

Yet terrorism is not the defining feature of Nigerian life. The firsthand accounts of young people demonstrate what everyday life can be like there. Nigerian children and teens have many of the same joys and frustrations that youth everywhere in the world experience.

A Day in the Life of Smartygirl10

In 2010, SparkLife, the blog of SparkNotes, published a Day in the Life post from a Nigerian ninth grader at an international K–12 school. She wrote under the online handle of smartygirl10.

Every day, smartygirl10's alarm went off at 7:00 a.m. Like most teens, she wrote, she usually struggled to get up. When she did, her morning routine included saying prayers. By 7:45, she'd be out the front door. Her family's driver took her to school. She wrote that most upper-class families in Nigeria, like hers, have drivers. The drivers' pay was and is relatively low. Every month, smartygirl10's family paid their driver around 15,000 naira, or $100.

Smartygirl10 lived only ten minutes from school, so she had time before the school day started at 8:00 a.m. to talk in the hall with her friends about Nigerian singers like Banky W and Wande Coal, who were popular then. They would catch up on Oyinbo (non-Nigerian) pop culture like Lady Gaga and the television show *Glee*. They would also discuss current events. When smartygirl10 wrote her post in 2010, Goodluck Jonathan had been president of Nigeria for only a few months. He had never been elected to a major public office. He had accepted the presidency after President Umaru Yar'Adua became ill and died. Smartygirl10 wrote that she and her friends would often talk about the new administration.

The thirty ninth-graders at smartygirl10's school all took math, business studies, computer and technical drawing, and economics in the morning. When the power went out

CANADIAN FORCES' OPERATION NABERIUS

French-speaking Canadian soldiers help train African militaries, including Nigeria's, in marksmanship (shooting); reconnaissance (observing an area in order to find the enemy); and other military skills. Since 2013, these skills have been focused primarily on stopping Boko Haram.

The Canadian soldiers are part of the Canadian Special Operation Regiment (CSOR). More specifically, they are members of Operation Naberius. This elite team is part of the United States' Exercise Flintlock, which has helped sixteen countries in West Africa fight terrorism. The operation does so by encouraging cooperation across the region, reducing the numbers of sanctuaries where terrorist organizations can safely hide, and training militaries. Flintlock has existed since 2005. It is led by the United States Chairman of the Joint Chiefs of Staff and US Africa Command.

According to the NATO Association of Canada (NAOC), Operation Naberius is part of a long-term plan for Canada supporting peace in Africa. As Africa's population grows, problems are also expected to rise, and more help will be needed. The United Nations has estimated that until 2050, more than half of the world's population growth will happen in Africa.

A Canadian soldier (kneeling) oversees a training exercise as part of Exercise Flintlock in 2017.

Not all those people will be educated or find good jobs. NAOC says this lack of opportunity will make many African countries "potential hotbed[s] for radical ideologies" that could lead to terror, just as Boko Haram's worldview has terrorized people now. NAOC also predicts that since many African countries use French, and French is also a national language of Canada, Canada has a responsibility to help more going forward.

during computer class, she called it a "normal occurrence" in Nigeria, even at her top-rated school.

The students would have a late-morning snack, and then they attended English and literature classes with the same instructor who taught economics. At lunch, smartygirl10 said nobody ate; they just caught up with friends in other classes.

In the afternoon was chemistry, smartygirl10's favorite class, and then PSAT prep, which helped them prepare for the pre-SAT standardized test they would take later that year. In Nigeria, the SAT is given in tenth grade.

School ended at 3:20 p.m. Lots of students were signed up for extracurricular activities. Smartygirl10 took Arabic for an hour after school. After that, she would do homework and a little television watching.

A Day in the Life of Dami Gilbert

US-born Nigerian American Dami Gilbert was a junior in high school in Minnesota in 2013 when she wrote about her experiences as a student in Lagos, Nigeria. She studied there during the 2010–2011 school year. ThreeSixty Journalism, a nonprofit program at the University of Saint Thomas in Minnesota, published her article as part of its mission to encourage teens from diverse backgrounds to work in journalism.

Dami's parents were born and raised in Nigeria but moved to the United States before Dami was born. After twenty-five years in the States, her parents decided to return to Nigeria to open and run businesses there. Dami went with them.

Like smartygirl10, Dami also started her school days at 7:00 a.m. Instead of a mechanical alarm, her mom and her dogs, Fedio and Douchess, woke her up. Also like smartygirl10, Dami did not welcome the sight of them. "Like the rest of the world," she writes, "I'm unhappy about going to school."

In her pink bedroom with its tile floor, Dami got dressed in her private-school uniform of burgundy skirt and white-and-burgundy-striped blouse. Her quality education was a luxury her parents could afford because their businesses were successful.

The family's maid greeted Dami in the kitchen, where she poured cereal for breakfast. Her dad helped her tie her burgundy tie before she slipped on her black shoes and headed outside. The day was warm even at that early hour; it was already seventy-six degrees Fahrenheit (about 24 degrees Celsius).

Like smartygirl10, Dami was taken to school by a driver, and she also did not have to go far. Her school was in the same gated community she lived in.

Dami's first academic class was chemistry, followed by English and literature. Morning break was called tea time. It was fifteen minutes for a snack and conversation with friends. Her morning continued with studying Yoruba, a Nigerian language, and French. As economics class ended, Dami wrote that she could smell the rice and chicken the "aunties" were cooking in the cafeteria for the students' lunch. In Nigeria, all elders are referred to as "aunties" and "uncles," as a sign of respect, even if they are not related to you.

Dami wrote a lot about how strict her school was. Each day started with an assembly. During assembly, teachers noted whether uniforms were ironed, shoes were polished, and fingernails were cut and unpainted. Girls had to have braided, uncolored, untreated hair. Boys had to keep their hair cut short. The punishment for breaking any of these rules was kneeling through classes all day or copying the longest verse in the Bible.

Dami noted that this expectation of perfection continued into classes. "I have a decent relationship with some of my teachers, but to be honest," she explained, "most of them scared me, which led me to hate their classes." Education in Nigeria revolves around memorization and drills. "Students are expected to learn and get the kind of rigorous education their parents paid for," she wrote. Even public schools cost money. This seriousness affects students, and they do not take school for granted. The majority of students respect their teachers as authority figures. Though Dami appreciated the sense of responsibility that comes from these factors, she writes that, ultimately, the anxiety of "never being good enough" and the fear that she would speak the wrong way to a teacher were too much for her. She returned to Minnesota for her final two years of high school.

Dami added that Nigerian school could be fun—at designated play times. Afternoon music class was fun. The school also celebrated holidays with decorations, dances, and parties. Sports are important in Nigeria, and often the male teachers would bring their soccer shoes on Fridays to join in the exercise.

A Day in the Life of Titi

Not all young people living in Nigeria are as fortunate as smartygirl10 and Dami. Titi was twelve years old when Al Jazeera told her story. Titi was born in the Republic of

Benin, a country to the west of Nigeria, but she was taken to Nigeria when she was ten years old. A person who worked as an "agent" convinced her family that she could earn money for them by working as a maid for a middle-class Nigerian family. Not every servant in Nigeria is coerced into working this young or in this way, but many people are so desperate for work that it does happen. The family Titi worked for paid the agent anywhere from six months' to two years' worth of salary. The agent promised to send it on to Titi's family, but there was no way of knowing if the agent did this or kept the money.

Like smartygirl10 and Dami, Titi woke at 7:00 a.m., but she began her day not with school but with sweeping and mopping. Eventually, her employers started sending her to school, but she had to finish her morning work before she walked the five minutes to school. After school, she worked again, often until 10:00 p.m., sometimes as late as 2:00 a.m.

Despite her difficult schedule, she told the newspaper that she hoped to remain with the family. She did not have the opportunity to go to school in Benin, and even though she was illiterate when she started school in Nigeria, she caught up in a few months and placed tenth in her class. She wanted to be a doctor.

As is the case in every country, in Nigeria, every teenager has his or her own experiences. Through smartygirl10's,

Dami's, and Titi's stories, we learned just three, but they help us to imagine life in a place that is in many ways similar to our own and in others quite different. The next chapter takes a closer look at Nigeria's history and how Boko Haram was able to take hold, ultimately threatening the day-to-day lives of many Nigerians.

Children play outside their school in Idanre, Nigeria. Boko Haram's rise is a threat to the young people of this beautiful nation.

CHAPTER TWO

THE RISE OF BOKO HARAM

Nigeria is a wonderful, complex, and important country. Boko Haram has taken advantage of the country's instability and its people's desperation to establish itself as one of the most violent terrorist organizations in the world. The many factors behind Boko Haram's rise include the scars of colonialism and religious strife.

Nigerian Independence

People have been living on the land that is now Nigeria for thousands of years. The Nok people settled the Jos plateau, at the center of modern-day Nigeria, around 800 BCE.

For about two thousand years, the population of the area grew, and the people formed states, kingdoms, and empires. In 1472, Europeans arrived by ship. The Portuguese were the first. From the 1500s to the 1700s, Europeans sent millions of Nigerians to the Americas to be slaves.

Nigeria's modern-day borders were drawn in 1914 as "an act of colonial convenience," according to Public Radio International (PRI). Britain had colonized both northern Nigeria and southern Nigeria and eventually decided it made sense to merge the two. That would form one powerfully placed territory, from the Sahel Desert in the north to the Atlantic Ocean in the south. It would also allow the more prosperous south to help fund the poorer north.

The colonists paid no attention to how different these two regions were. They did not care what the people who had lived there for generations thought about uniting—and what they thought was not positive. Most residents of northern Nigeria practice Islam and align themselves culturally with the Middle East and the wider Muslim world. Islam came to Nigeria in 1809, and the north was Islam's home base in that part of the world. Ethnically diverse southern Nigerians follow Christianity, as well as some of the traditions of the West and other parts of Africa. In so many ways, the north and the south behave as different countries. Being forced to act as one has caused serious internal turmoil. According to

PRI, one leader from the north called Nigeria "the mistake of 1914."

It did not help that Britain's ruling style forced Nigerians to take sides against each other. Indirect rule left day-to-day ruling to community leaders, with British oversight. If a person identified with the "correct" religion or ethnicity, in the eyes of the British, they received more political and economic resources. If there were no local leaders satisfactory to the colonizers, the British chose, often selecting leadership the citizens did not agree with.

By the time Nigeria started trying to win its independence from Britain, it had been one country for decades. It could not easily choose to be two countries because it now had ties as one. From 1947 to 1959, leaders representing Nigeria's different regions, ethnicities, and religions negotiated their freedom and how they could rule themselves, together. They declared the country's independence in 1960.

A Young Nigerian's Winning Design

For a long time, the country that would become known as Nigeria was ruled by European outsiders. Even its name was determined by someone external. Flora Shaw was a British journalist (for a time, the highest-paid female in journalism) who was the first to call the territories administered by the Royal Niger Company by one name: Nigeria.

So, when Nigeria won its independence in the mid-twentieth century, it would be a source of pride that a Nigerian ended up designing the country's new flag. In 1958, Michael Taiwo Akinkunmi was a twenty-three-year-old engineering student in London. He was born in Ibadan, today Nigeria's most sprawling urban center and third–most populous city. As a young person excited for his country to be free again, Akinkunmi answered the public call for a design contest for a new national flag for Nigeria. In October 1959, he was notified that his green-and-white design had been selected. He was paid the equivalent of $281. For a time, he was famous. "I was well-known all over the place," Akinkunmi told Al Jazeera in 2015. "Everybody was calling me Mr. Flag Man."

Akinkunmi had loved his country his whole life, despite hardships. When he was an elderly man and living back in Nigeria, a historian visited him to learn about his life. "He would never say anything negative," the scholar told Al Jazeera, even though he was struggling. "He would say 'God bless Nigeria,' or 'Nigeria is moving forward and will keep moving forward.'"

Turmoil After Unification

Peaceful unification of Nigeria did not last long. So much controversy surrounded the first census after independence,

A young soldier keeps watch during the war between Nigeria and Biafra in the late 1960s.

in 1962, that the prime minister called for a redo in 1963. The main fight was between northern and southern Nigeria. The census showed how many people lived in each part of the country. Regions received representation in the government based on how many people lived there. Political power was an incentive to have a correct count.

Two of Nigeria's major ethnic groups are the Hausa-Fulani, who live in the northern part of the country, and the Igbo, who now hail from southeastern Nigeria. In 1966, Muslim Hausas began massacring Christian Igbos in the north. Survivors fled to eastern Nigeria. Most of the country's Igbo ethnic group lived in the east, and they feared the national government would crack down on their growing power base. Therefore, in 1967, several eastern states broke away from Nigeria to form the Republic of Biafra. For two and a half years, war between Nigeria and Biafra destroyed the east. In 1970, the country reunited.

These events—plus ongoing general mismanagement of the country's natural resources and lingering negative effects of Britain's identity politics—served to deepen each religion's suspicion of the other. Christians blamed Muslims for Nigeria's problems, and Muslims blamed Christians. According to PRI, "this genuine, if misplaced, quest for a religious utopia has given some opportunistic political gladiators an excuse to curry legitimacy through politicized appeals to piety and religious fervor." In other words, people were pitting one religion against the other, saying members of one were bad while those of the other were good. They were trying to find "religious solutions to socioeconomic and political problems." Those solutions would help some people and exclude others, or at least be perceived as favoring one group over another.

For example, starting in 2000, much of northern Nigeria adopted the sharia criminal legal system. Christian minority groups living there protested out of fear that they would be persecuted. Islamic religious rules had replaced secular rules as the region's official legal system, but not everyone living there followed Islam. Violence between groups began happening regularly in northern Nigeria. Southern Nigeria often became involved, too, because majority Christian groups there wanted to support their members who lived as minority populations in the north. Christians in the south also retaliated against Muslim actions in the north by attacking their own southern Muslim neighbors.

Boko Haram

Boko Haram is a Nigerian-based terror organization that grew out of this instability in 2002. Boko Haram's members kill citizens, kidnap them, destroy entire villages, and force even young children to fight for them. They do all this in

CHRIS ABANI

Chris Abani is a novelist, poet, and publisher. His first novel was published when he was sixteen years old. *Masters of the Board* is a thriller about an attempted Nigerian coup. A coup is the forcible removal of a country's leadership from power. Around the time the book was published, a real coup almost happened. It was very different from the coup Abani imagined for his book, which included neo-Nazis, a Nigerian

Chris Abani poses for a photo in 2007.

James Bond–type character named Coyote Williams, and action that spanned four continents. Still, the Nigerian government believed Abani's novel had encouraged the actual coup, so they threw him in prison when he was only eighteen years old. That was the first of three times the government imprisoned Abani.

Abani was born in 1966 to a privileged family. His mother was from England, and his parents had met as students at the University of Oxford. When the Biafran-Nigerian civil war started, Abani's mother took her five children from refugee camp to refugee camp, slowly moving them out of the country to Portugal and then on to England. At every refugee camp, she had to prevent soldiers from taking her oldest son, who was nine years old, to serve with them. When the war ended, they returned to Nigeria.

In spite of the consequences, Abani always kept writing. American author Dave Eggers once wrote, "Chris Abani might be the most courageous writer working right now. There is no subject matter he finds daunting, no challenge he fears. Aside from that, he's stunningly prolific and writes like an angel. If you want to get at the molten heart of contemporary fiction, Abani is the starting point." Today, Abani lives and teaches in the United States.

the name of religion, though experts see their beliefs not as part of any religion but as part of a terrifying and incorrect interpretation of religion.

What's in a Name?

Boko Haram is a nickname for the group's official name, Jamāʿat Ahl al-Sunna lil-Daʿawah wa al-Jihād. This means The People Committed to the Propagation of the Prophet's Teachings and Jihad. The "propagation of the prophet's teachings" means that the group is interested in spreading the holy word of the founder of Islam, the prophet Muhammad. It is also interested in fighting people and nations considered enemies of Islam, or waging a jihad. The name Boko Haram means "Western education is forbidden" or "Westernization is sacrilege."

Boko Haram's Philosophy

The philosophical foundation for Boko Haram came from outside of Nigeria. In the mid-1990s, Muhammad Yusuf was a young Nigerian Islamic cleric learning about Wahhabism, a branch of Islam that started in Saudi Arabia in the 1700s. Its followers are devoted to what they consider a pure form of Islam and reject modern ways, including any education that does not center around religion. These views have led to extremist actions. In 2013, the European Parliament in Strasbourg called Wahhabism "the main source of global terrorism."

Inspired by Wahhabism, Yusuf declared that Muslims in his country should overthrow Nigeria's secular government and replace it with an Islamic one. For several years, the government saw Yusuf's Boko Haram as just an anomaly and an annoyance in the northeast part of Nigeria.

The 2009 Turning Point

By 2009, the government was alarmed that Boko Haram was growing stronger, adding members and stockpiling weapons. The government decided to remind the group that it, not Boko Haram, was still in charge. Police stopped a Boko Haram motorcycle funeral procession to ticket the riders for not wearing helmets. Fights broke out, leaving several people wounded.

Yusuf ordered his people to retaliate. For several days, they attacked government and police buildings across five northern Nigerian states. They even broke into a prison and freed people. In turn, the government increased the severity of its response. The national military executed suspected

Boko Haram militants in the street. Yusuf was taken into custody and killed. At the hands of both sides, more than one thousand people died over those few days.

The government banned Boko Haram from the country, sending members into hiding. The quiet would last only a few months. Boko Haram started invading villages again, trying to gain territory in the historically Muslim-majority northern states. At the same time, they worked to eliminate everyone who wasn't Muslim from the country. They sought to convert the entire country's legal system to sharia law. They bombed churches when they were full of worshippers. They bombed political offices and killed people running for office. They even attacked the United Nations offices in Abuja, Nigeria, killing more than twenty people and injuring eighty. The country's military tried to stop them, but they found themselves up against a prepared enemy.

Supported by Money and Corruption

Boko Haram is not an incredibly wealthy, all-powerful organization. However, it has been better supported than the Nigerian military. This is interesting because the Nigerian military supposedly has the country's full resources at its disposal. These resources include donations from other countries as well as internal support. For example, in

May 2016, the British government said it was giving Nigeria $52 million over the next four years to fight Boko Haram. In May 2017, the Nigerian government approved a $440 million budget for its Ministry of Defense. In contrast, the United Nations Security Council's Counter-Terrorism Committee estimates Boko Haram has an annual budget of around $10 million. Yet, also according to the United Nations and reported by *Newsweek*, Nigerian soldiers have gone to battle armed with AK-47s only, while Boko Haram has met them with "rocket-propelled grenades, machine guns with anti-aircraft visors, automatic rifles, grenades, and explosives."

Transparency International, which is an organization that monitors corruption around the world, found that elites inside and outside of the Nigerian government have inflated or faked military contracts and then kept the money for themselves. They have hidden the money outside of Nigeria, often in Western countries. Their greed hurts the Nigerian military and gives Boko Haram more power.

Western governments have taken some steps to remedy corruption. In March 2016, US Secretary of State John Kerry pledged to trace what he agreed was likely billions of dollars embezzled from Nigeria and hidden in the US financial system. In 2017, the US government sued Kola Aluko, a wealthy Nigerian with American ties, to try to recover some of Nigeria's money. He was accused of buying yachts and New York City penthouses and partying with Hollywood celebrities with money from a $1.76 billion scam involving the Nigerian government and profits from oil sales. Also in 2017, anticorruption experts started exposing Nigerian money hidden in Great Britain with a unique bus tour through London. The bus, filled with journalists and other advocates, stopped at properties purchased with embezzled money. Many are empty. They are purchased with stolen money to conceal the money as property. One of the tour guides told Agence France-Presse, an international news agency, that "London had become the 'Death Star' of global kleptocracy, which he defined as the stealing, hiding and spending of public money." The West was playing a key role in Nigeria's corruption.

Wanting More Power

Experts worry that Boko Haram may want to expand its territory by aligning itself with other terror organizations, like ISIS. Boko Haram is already expanding its territory beyond Nigeria's borders, because country borders do not halt the spread of violence. In fact, Boko Haram's efforts in Nigeria have been focused near the country's borders with Niger, Chad, and Cameroon, in what is known as the Lake

Chad area. Naturally, Boko Haram's violence spills over into and affects these neighbors.

In 2015, Boko Haram pledged its allegiance to ISIS. In 2016, the US military said it witnessed "one of the first concrete examples of a direct link between the two extremist groups," according to the *New York Times*. A weapons convoy likely sent by ISIS militants in Libya was intercepted on its way to the Lake Chad region, a territory controlled by Boko Haram. A few months later, ISIS further confirmed its connection to Boko Haram by announcing the Nigerian group had a new leader, Abu Musab al-Barnawi.

Interestingly, Boko Haram distanced itself from ISIS's comment. Shekau, who had led Boko Haram since 2009, quickly released a statement saying that ISIS was incorrect and that he was still in charge. He called al-Barnawi "an infidel," someone who believes the wrong faith. He also said that ISIS's announcement should be considered a type of coup.

Shekau Introduces a New Level of Violence and Revenge

Because few people have seen Shekau, analysts cautioned people from believing any announcements supposedly made by him. However, experts said it made sense that ISIS would want to replace Shekau. Under his leadership, Boko Haram militants target mosques and Muslims, not just churches and Christians. This concerns ISIS, which sees the world as Muslims versus everyone else. Shekau, however, leads Boko Haram terrorists to target anyone working against him and in favor of democracy and education beyond schooling in Islam.

In 2015, Muhammadu Buhari ran for president of Nigeria partially on the promise to do more to stop Boko Haram. In a February 2015 video, Shekau warned that he would go after anyone, including Muslims, who voted for Buhari. "The reason why I will kill you is you are infidels, you follow democracy," Shekau said, as reported by the *Daily Beast*. "Whoever follows democracy is an infidel."

Buhari won the election. The day after he was sworn into office, a bomb exploded in a mosque near a popular market. Twenty-seven people died, and more than thirty were hurt. The mosque was destroyed. Boko Haram continued to attack Muslim sites as revenge for the election of Buhari. Boko Haram's attacks coincided with the Muslim holy days of Ramadan, which meant mosques were more full than usual. Over the course of just one day in July, Boko Haram militants killed 150 people in mosques as well as people at home in three rural Muslim-majority villages. By the time Ramadan ended, Boko Haram had murdered three hundred Nigerian Muslims.

Challenges Ahead

From being an ancient land of royalty, to a modern country brimming with brilliance, possibility, and strife, Nigeria is a fascinating place. Unfortunately, it is losing generations of its people to the terrorist organization Boko Haram. In the next chapter, we'll meet some of those lost: Nigeria's child soldiers of Boko Haram.

In 2015, Nigeria's military displayed a poster of the most-wanted Boko Haram militants.

CHAPTER THREE

TEEN RECRUITS

In a report it published in 2016, international humanitarian organization Mercy Corps found that it is impossible to neatly categorize the reasons why young people join Boko Haram. When experiencing uncertainty and feeling threatened by violence, anyone, but especially young people, will understandably feel confused about how to make the best choices for themselves and their loved ones. When Mercy Corps asked young people why they became soldiers for Boko Haram, the researchers "heard stories that blended elements of coercion and elements of volition, and very often, it was a series of small events or circumstances that led a youth to become part of the group."

Child Soldiers Around the World and in Boko Haram: By the Numbers

Militaries, rebel groups, and terrorist organizations around the world recruit, coerce, or abduct young people to work for them. It is nearly impossible to know how many people are, or have been, child soldiers. Armed groups are secretive about their membership for numerous reasons: they are often committing illegal acts, or their members may be shunned by their communities if their identities are revealed. Also, these groups operate during periods of great instability. It is difficult to conduct accurate, comprehensive research in war zones or regions devastated by economic strife or political turmoil. In such chaos, it is difficult to know if missing children are acting as soldiers or if they have run away or been injured or even killed.

As a result, experts must estimate how many young people have been directly involved with militaries, rebel groups, and terrorist organizations. Based on what firsthand accounts they do have, some experts guess that there are three hundred thousand to five hundred thousand child soldiers serving around the world at any one time. Another means of estimation is examining related data. For example, between

2007 and 2017, sixty-five thousand children were released from working for armed groups, according to UNICEF. This number does not tell us what year the youth joined or how long they served, but it does give a sense of the enormity of the problem.

Even though so many children have been released from armed groups, many others remain and continue to join. Some people estimate that Boko Haram has forced into service ten thousand boys since the organization began in 2002.

Recruiting Child Soldiers Is Illegal

Armed groups allow youth to serve even though doing so breaks international law. Generally, children are not allowed to serve in state-run or nonstate militaries. In 2000, the Optional Protocol on the Involvement of Children in Armed Conflict (OPAC) was added to the Convention on the Rights of the Child. This was the first treaty to focus on ending military exploitation of people under age eighteen throughout the world. People charged with using youth as soldiers can be taken to court. The International Criminal Court (ICC), created in 2002, is the first permanent court investigating and trying cases on a global level. It judges individuals charged with "the gravest crimes of concern to the international community," like genocide and war crimes. According to the Rome Statute, an international treaty that guides the court in its decision-making, recruiting or requiring people who are younger than fifteen is not just illegal—it is a war crime.

The Definitions of "Child" and "Child Soldier" Around the World and in Nigeria

The legal definition of "child" is sometimes a person as young as fifteen, but usually the term means a person no older than eighteen. Nigeria considers young people to be between the ages of eighteen and thirty-five. So, when Mercy Corps decided to study Boko Haram's child soldiers, its researchers followed Nigeria's age guidelines. From September to November 2015, they interviewed forty-seven people who had been members of Boko Haram when they were younger. Some of the people they interviewed had been as young as sixteen years old when they entered Boko Haram.

The definition of "child soldier" extends beyond being "a young person who fights with weapons." Child soldiers or members of an armed group are young people who actively participate in some way. Some Boko Haram child soldiers fight in battles (often being sent to the front lines because they are seen as good distractions and as expendable), but many cook for the adult soldiers and clean the camps, spy on the enemy, or recruit others to continue to grow Boko Haram's ranks. They may be used as low-ranking scavengers and be sent into a village after the adult soldiers have burned or otherwise destroyed it. These children and teens may be tasked with picking through the rubble for anything of value to steal. They may also hold roles of incredible importance that bring them into close contact with Boko Haram leaders and their plans. If a young soldier has had more schooling than an adult leader, he may be asked to help the leader read communications. Sometimes the tasks may seem boring and not much different from chores around home, but there is nothing safe about this life.

Child Soldiers in Boko Haram

Boko Haram was unique in that, as of 2016, most of its thousands of members were youth. In 2016 alone, UNICEF estimated that it recruited two thousand children to join. Boko Haram's young members are themselves unique. The

2016 report by Mercy Corps demonstrates this. Mercy Corps interviewed twenty-six males and twenty-one females who joined Boko Haram as youth. These young soldiers came from the Borno, Yobe, and Gombe states in northeast Nigeria. These are the areas most affected by Boko Haram. In 2013, the Nigerian government declared states of emergency in Borno and Yobe.

Stories from Ex-Soldiers Provide New Information

Discussing Boko Haram is scary and dangerous. Mercy Corps researchers had no way of knowing how forthcoming, open, and honest the respondents were being. They might have feared being found and hurt by Boko Haram if they revealed secrets. They might have worried about being shunned by their families, who could be horrified by their actions while they were involved with the terrorist organization.

The information in the report is useful. It is some of the only available data on Boko Haram members from primary sources—the ex-soldiers themselves. "Despite widespread devastation linked to Boko Haram," the Mercy Corps report explained, "lack of access due to insecurity has prevented a deep understanding of participation in the group."

Basic Demographics

One of the first things that researchers from Mercy Corps learned about Boko Haram child recruits was that they could not guess based on background who would join the organization and who would not. Mercy Corps interviewed people who joined Boko Haram before the militant group became well known in 2009 and those who joined after. All but one left the group voluntarily. Some had little education before they joined, and some had graduated from college. The same number had completed Islamic school as had completed a secular, nonreligious education. Some had jobs, and some did not; some had been popular in their communities, and some had had few friends before joining Boko Haram.

Reasons to Join Boko Haram: Religion

All of the people Mercy Corps interviewed identified as Muslim, though not all practiced their faith regularly. Mercy Corps' research refuted the assumption that most Boko Haram youth came from Islamic Tsangaya schools. Almajirai, the name for those religion students, immerse themselves in Islamic education by living with their teachers, but that does not mean they want to convert others to Islam through violence. There is no logical connection between those two things.

BOKO HARAM ON TWITTER

Boko Haram joined Twitter in early 2015. This indicated an important change in the organization. In the twenty-first century, even terrorist groups need to be on social media to stay relevant and to build up their membership. By joining Twitter, Boko Haram was indicating that it was ready to be bigger and stronger.

Boko Haram members also started using YouTube. Before, they physically couriered videos to journalists. With YouTube, they switched to uploading videos. Old videos were in the Nigerian language of Hausa only. New videos were subtitled in Arabic and English. These changes indicated Boko Haram wanted to start publicizing their propaganda to a global audience.

Experts wondered if this also indicated Boko Haram not only wanted to copy ISIS's impressive social media skills but also formally align with the Islamic State terrorist group. Within the next two years, the two groups did start working together more closely.

Boko Haram's online attempts have not been entirely successful. The group was not skilled at linking its social media accounts so that all projected the same message at the same

A. F. Branco's political cartoon says that "hashtag activism" doesn't scare Boko Haram, unless there's action taken to back up that activism.

time. There were also serious quality issues. According to Terrorism Monitor, members publicly complained about difficulty finding fast and reliable internet connection to upload their messages. Twitter, YouTube, and other social media platforms also occasionally remove content or accounts believed to be related to Boko Haram, which violate the platforms' terms of service because the group promotes violence.

A young girl observes a Muslim holiday in Lagos in 2017. There is a large difference between Boko Haram's brand of Islam and true Islam, like hers.

Still, of those who joined Boko Haram before 2009, religion was often an important part of their recruitment story. One young man said, "They told us that it is the role of youth to protect the religion of God." Girls and young women were interested in joining because Boko Haram offered them the religious education they desired but were not always allowed to have. Islam teaches that everyone should know its holy book, the Quran, but Nigerian society does not prioritize the education of girls. The girls who do attend often drop out because of marriage or pregnancy.

Once Shekau became leader in 2009 and redirected the group in a more violent direction, many young people did not stay interested in Boko Haram's religious talk. "They were not ultimately convinced that the Boko Haram brand of Islam was the right one," the Mercy Corps report said.

Reasons to Join Boko Haram: Business Security

Militaries, rebel groups, and terrorist organizations around the world who recruit young people often target those who are living in desperate economic situations. If a young person does not have a job or the education to obtain a job, or if the adults in their family are not working, the young person may see being a soldier as a way to save themselves and their family. Armed groups often promise financial compensation.

In contrast, many Nigerian youth told Mercy Corps that they ran small businesses but still joined Boko Haram. They did so to secure loans, so they could improve their businesses, or they were forced to join when they could not repay loans Boko Haram had already given them.

Some young people pledged their allegiance to Boko Haram for protection. One young man explained that when the group started terrorizing towns near his, he joined up. When Boko Haram came to his town, his family's home was the only one not burned. Other young people felt pressured by their customers or their bosses to listen to Boko Haram.

The myth has been that young people joined Boko Haram to escape poverty. Most people in Nigeria, 61 percent of the population, live in extreme poverty, so this theory seemed viable. However, Mercy Corps found no relationship between the two. The humanitarian organization did find a correlation regarding inequality, and economics can be a factor in inequality. Relative deprivation can make youth vulnerable to recruitment. Relative deprivation can be defined as the gap between what people think they deserve and what they think they will actually receive. Regarding money, Nigeria is wildly unequal. In the northeast, Boko Haram's home territory, more than 76 percent of the population lives in absolute poverty. In the southwest, which has always been resource-wealthy, only 59 percent are impoverished. People definitely could feel frustrated that they do not have what their neighbors have.

Reasons to Join Boko Haram: Obligation

Peer pressure mattered to boys and girls. If someone important to a young person was involved with Boko Haram, that person was more likely to join than someone who did not have loved ones or respected role models in the group.

Women and girls play an active role in Boko Haram campaigns, and most do not volunteer to join. Rather, they feel obliged to join their husbands, or are coerced to, or are abducted. Amnesty International reported that Boko Haram kidnapped two thousand females, including young girls, between early 2014 and April 2015.

There are always exceptions to the rule. Mercy Corps' report stresses that Nigerian girls and women should not be considered to be completely lacking in agency when faced with Boko Haram. Some engage in "meaningful dialogue" with their friends and husbands about Boko Haram's philosophy and ideology. Sometimes, they are even the persuasive ones in a marriage and encourage their husbands to join along with them.

Reasons to Join Boko Haram: Frustration with the Government

Government corruption left Nigerians, including young people, looking beyond their elected officials for leadership. Boko Haram took advantage of people's frustration. People interviewed spoke of Boko Haram as potential peacemakers.

Some said they believed that Boko Haram would stamp out government corruption and prioritize their religious values.

Kidnapping Youth

The most terrifying way many young people "join" Boko Haram is by being kidnapped and forced to serve. Not only is the situation violent and terrifying for them, but often their families are left wondering what happened to them and if they will ever see their children again.

Sometimes the kidnapping begins as an at-home imprisonment. For example, in 2014, Boko Haram took over a Nigerian town and held three hundred students, age seven to seventeen, in a school there for months. Finally, they drove away with the children and teenagers. This transport is as terrifying as every other part of the kidnapping; young people are often piled into trucks and not allowed fresh air or water.

Escaping Boko Haram

There are usually only three ways out of a nonstate military like Boko Haram: being rescued by a group like the state-run military, dying, or escaping. The first way is unlikely and uncertain. Especially in big countries like Nigeria, with diverse terrain, unstable political conditions, and questionable infrastructure, it is difficult to locate, track, and successfully and safely apprehend all units of Boko Haram. The second way out, dying, is a terrible tragedy. The third way, escaping, is extremely dangerous. It is difficult to sneak away from watchful commanders. If a child soldier manages to get away, he or she must then survive in the wild possibly far from home or any safe village.

Perpetrators and Victims

The young people interviewed by Mercy Corps about their time in Boko Haram were all survivors. However, they have all been forever affected by their trauma, and many of their friends did not escape or survive. In many ways, even though they carry out terrible acts, child soldiers of Boko Haram are themselves victims of the terrorist group. The next chapter discusses other young casualties: those killed, displaced from their homes, and held hostage by Boko Haram.

CHIBOK STUDENTS INSPIRE A SUPERHERO

Ngozi is a teenage superhero who fights evil in Lagos, Nigeria. In September 2017, she became the newest member of the Marvel Comics Venomverse universe. She is based on real-life brave teens, the girls kidnapped from their school in Chibok by Boko Haram in 2014.

Nnedi Okorafor is the Nigerian American science-fiction writer and English professor who is writing Ngozi's story. It is called "Blessing in Disguise." She told the BBC that life for Ngozi is normal … until she goes outside to catch a grasshopper, and her whole world changes. Similarly, she told Reuters, the Chibok students "were normal girls who suddenly had to deal with a huge change in their lives … and their story of perseverance is so powerful."

Okorafor showed the artist working on her comic several photos of the kidnapped girls and asked her to draw Ngozi in their likeness. Okorafor told the BBC that by setting her story in Lagos, "it practically writes itself." She said, "Lagos is awesome! Lagos is full of life and vibrancy and action and adventure and story."

Nnedi Okorafor is the writer behind the Nigerian superhero Ngozi, a Marvel Comics character.

Okorafor told Reuters that she wanted to encourage more diversity in comics in terms of race and gender as well as geography and situation. She succeeded. Ngozi is Marvel's first Nigerian superhero. Her story is the first time the major comics publisher is setting a story in a real African country.

Okorafor hoped Ngozi would "resonate with girls" across Nigeria. She told Reuters, "Like many Nigerian girls, Ngozi comes in a small package but is strong-willed and determined."

A Boko Haram camp in Borno State, Nigeria, in 2016. Boko Haram's victims are sometimes forced to live in camps like this one.

CHAPTER FOUR

THE YOUNGEST CASUALTIES OF BOKO HARAM

Boko Haram is a homegrown, localized terror organization. Despite its singular focus, it has caused a lot of long-lasting damage in Nigeria and its neighboring countries. As of 2016, Boko Haram had been responsible for the deaths of nearly seventeen thousand people, the displacement of nearly 2.2 million people, and the destruction of countless communities, villages, and cities. There are many ways that Boko Haram has destroyed lives. This chapter looks at three groups of young people who have suffered because of the militant group: they are human weapons, displaced people and refugees, and kidnapped hostages.

DIFFERENT RESPONSES TO SIMILAR TERROR ATTACKS

For seventy-two hours in January 2015, Paris, France, was on lockdown. Three men wearing hoods that covered their faces entered the offices of *Charlie Hebdo*, a magazine that publishes satire there. The men began shooting guns. Later, in another part of the metropolitan area, an armed man took hostages in a grocery store in a neighborhood known for its large Jewish community. By the time police had controlled both situations, seventeen people were dead, as were the three attackers.

Nigeria was experiencing terror at the same time. Over the course of one week, Boko Haram killed as many as two thousand people. Militants stormed towns in northern Nigeria and shot their guns at anyone they saw. They ran after people who tried to hide. They set fires to homes. Some of the people forced to do the killing on behalf of Boko Haram were children. Those who survived were displaced from their destroyed villages. At least thirty thousand people had to move suddenly. Amnesty International called the attack Boko Haram's deadliest.

The attacks in Paris received an immediate international response. People started using the hashtag #JeSuisCharlie. This translates to "I am Charlie." It references the name of the

The *Charlie Hebdo* offices after the bombing in 2011

magazine, *Charlie Hebdo*, and indicates solidarity with victims of terror. In contrast, Boko Haram's attack did not get much attention outside of Nigeria. There are many reasons for this. These include the general public perception that "bad things" happen in places like Africa, not Western Europe. There are fewer news crews on the ground in rural Nigeria than in urban France. The Paris attacks were also symbolic, as the gunmen were in part lashing out against freedom of the press, a right that many people in the world hold dear as a part of basic human freedom.

Human Weapons

Boko Haram may not be the most well-funded terrorist organization, but its members put what resources they have to terrifying use. In 2016, General Lamidi Oyebayo Adeosun spoke during a US press conference about his work as the Nigerian commander of the regional group of African countries fighting Boko Haram. He showed photos of the bombs Boko Haram had invented. One was a live bird wrapped in explosives that the militants could get into crowds easily. However, that was far from the scariest thing Boko Haram has done with bombs. The worst involves children.

Boko Haram, Adeosun said, is using children—especially girls, some as young as eight—to carry bombs into crowded areas. "They are appealing to the natural care you feel for a girl child," the *New York Times* reported the general as saying. "When you see a girl child, you will not feel that she could be carrying a bomb. They achieve maximum effect that way." Toby Lanzer, the United Nations humanitarian coordinator covering Nigeria, called it the "epitome of evil" and said he could think of nothing "more horrifying," the *New York Times* reported.

Between 2014 and 2016, one in every five Boko Haram suicide bombers was a child. The number is growing. In 2014, the terrorist group used children in four such attacks; the next year, they used forty-four children.

A witness to a December 2016 attack like this, which killed one and injured seventeen, explained what he saw. Two girls about seven or eight years old "got out of a rickshaw and walked right in front of me without showing the slightest sign of emotion," the man told United Press International. "I tried to speak with one of them, in Hausa and in English, but she didn't answer. I thought they were looking for their mother. She headed toward the poultry sellers, then detonated her explosives belt." Boko Haram has been known to drug its soldiers to make them do as they are ordered. If these girls were drugged, that may explain their lack of emotion.

Sometimes, girls who are being held captive by Boko Haram volunteer to carry the bombs. Fati, who was kidnapped when she was thirteen and freed by Cameroonian soldiers when she was fifteen, told UNICEF Australia that many girls she knew in the Boko Haram camps wanted this assignment "because they wanted to go to the army and have them remove the belts. That way they would escape." They thought that as soon as they were in public, someone would help them. Tragically, some of the explosives are detonated not by the children wearing them but by Boko Haram soldiers far away, who use remote controls. The children were physically away from their captors, but they still could not escape.

Refugees

Though Boko Haram has tried to align itself with international terrorist powerhouses like ISIS, it has remained primarily a threat in one country, Nigeria. Within Nigeria, its focus has been the northeast, close to the country's borders with Cameroon, Chad, and Niger. This has naturally involved those other three countries, Cameroon particularly. The Kanuri ethnic group, which most Boko Haram members belong to, live in both Nigeria and Cameroon.

Between March 2014 and August 2017, Boko Haram led at least 510 attacks in Cameroon. At the same time, tens of thousands of Nigerians, displaced from their homes because of Boko Haram's actions in their country, found shelter in Cameroon. For half a century, Cameroon had been known as a generous refuge for people in need from all over the continent. Now, Boko Haram crossing the border to attack villages in Cameroon has made that country's government start worrying about its security.

In response, Human Rights Watch (HRW) reported, Cameroon has begun returning Nigerian refugees to Nigeria. From early 2015 to mid-2017, Cameroon sent one hundred thousand Nigerians back to Borno state. During this process, children were separated from their parents. Forcing refugees to go back defies the 2016 request by the Office of the United Nations High Commissioner for Refugees (UNHCR) that no one be returned to northeastern Nigeria because it was neither secure nor safe. HRW reported that the Cameroonian government pressured the Nigerian government into sending its own military vehicles to collect one thousand Nigerians. Nigeria therefore "became complicit in the unlawful forced return of its own citizens," HRW wrote.

Still, Nigerians continued to try to escape Boko Haram by going to Cameroon. The border checks at Cameroon became severe. Sometimes, the Cameroon army abused the asylum seekers. In June 2016, Cameroon, Chad, Niger, and Nigeria adopted the Abuja Action Statement. This agreement committed them to addressing to the needs of children at risk because of the region's violence. It said the countries would watch out for, and protect, children without parents and children being forced to do things against their will. Additionally, the countries would offer young people services like therapy. Days later, Cameroon seemingly violated this agreement by deporting 338 Nigerians, mostly women and children.

The refugee camps for Nigerians in Cameroon are becoming dangerous. They have restricted food and water, according to the 2017 report by HRW.

An eighteen-year-old-woman told HRW that even when they had access to food, soldiers often prevented them from gathering wood with which to cook it. She said the soldiers would beat them and demand bribes. Not only were they not getting their firewood, but they were being threatened with being detained. An eighteen-year-old young man told HRW that he saw Cameroonian soldiers in his camp who were "frequently drunk," and they "assaulted refugees … for no apparent reason." A nineteen-year-old young woman living in another Cameroon refuge told HRW that soldiers "took advantage of women" and "took away lots of men and women as Boko Haram suspects." Three of her friends had unwanted pregnancies because the soldiers forced them into relationships.

Kidnappings

In 2014, HRW published a report about the five hundred girls kidnapped by Boko Haram from northern Nigeria in the previous five years. One of the most famous was the kidnapping of more than two hundred high school students in Chibok, northeastern Nigeria. Part of the reason that kidnapping made international news was because of how many young women were taken and how long they remained in captivity. In total, 276 teens were taken, and 57 escaped

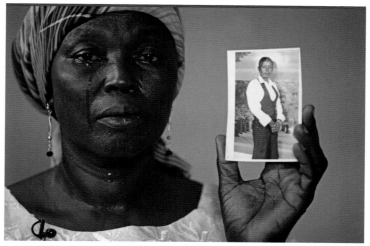
In this 2014 photo, Martha Mark holds a picture of her daughter, Monica, who was kidnapped in Chibok.

within hours of their abduction. Three and a half years after the kidnapping, 113 were still missing.

The Chibok kidnapping was hardly the only mass kidnapping that Boko Haram has carried out, and that is another reason the Chibok event made the news. It was a clear example of the fact that no one seemed to be safe anywhere in Nigeria. While doing chores at home or studying for exams in school, a person could be a target of Boko Haram. Two days after the Chibok students were taken, Boko Haram kidnapped eight other young women and girls from their village. Then, nine days later, five more from a different town. Boko Haram seemed to grow ever bolder. Eleven teenagers disappeared in May. In June, Boko Haram gunmen were seen taking sixty young women. Despite the fact that women

MORE REFUGEES THAN LOCALS

As of 2015, Boko Haram's violent actions had internally displaced 1.5 million Nigerians. As the militants swept through towns, killing people and destroying property, civilians fled their homes.

The Nigerian government could not keep up with the need for temporary emergency shelter and other resources. The *Guardian* reported that the director of the emergency management organization in the country's most affected state did not even have a computer in his office. In other words, resources were sorely lacking. Only a small percentage of people in need in the country's most affected state have found housing in the state's five official camps and fifteen "'camp-like' settlements," the *Guardian* reported. "This has left ordinary citizens to rally together in search of a safe haven."

Regular citizens opened schools, mosques, churches, and homes to internally displaced people (IDPs). A priest told the *Guardian*, "The numbers are so overwhelming that what we're giving is a drop compared to the needs." In the state's capital, Yola, IDPs began to outnumber the four hundred thousand people who permanently lived there.

Women who have been internally displaced carry food in 2014.

Though they receive much goodwill from their neighbors, these IDPs are also earning their own keep. Monica and her eight children fled their farm and now live with fourteen other people in a donated, unfinished, windowless house in Yola. Every day, she sends her older children to sell plastic bags of water in the street. With the proceeds from forty sold bags, they can buy one tube of toothpaste.

and girls are kidnapping targets, "very little is known about the abuses endured by women and girls in captivity," the HRW report explained.

Reasons for Kidnapping

By kidnapping young people, Boko Haram was moving from attacking politicians and other authorities who represented secular, not Islamic, rule. They seemed to want to hit communities where it would hurt most, by taking their females, who were vulnerable, innocent, and very important to communities. The first time Boko Haram abducted a whole group of young women and girls, not just one person, was in May 2013. Boko Haram leader Abubakar Shekau released a video explaining, "We kidnapped some women and children, including teenage girls … No one in the country will enjoy his women and children" until the state police released Boko Haram relatives from custody.

Another motivation might be punishment. Boko Haram members were targeting girls because they were attending school, and members of the terrorist organization consider non-Islamic education sinful. A nineteen-year-old told HRW that she was kidnapped while driving home from school with four friends. Boko Haram had set up a road block and was demanding the identity of each person who tried to pass.

The militant who stopped the girls soon learned they were students. He held them for two days because education was "sinful." They were released only after promising to never return to school.

A third possibility for Boko Haram's interest in kidnapping civilians was that they wanted to convert Christians to Islam. A twenty-three-year-old talked with HRW about being abducted, along with her mother, from her village. They were taken to a house outside of town. Four other kidnap victims, all teenagers, were already there. The Boko Haram leader there said the hostages were going to convert them to Islam, and then each of them was going to marry a soldier. The young woman and her mother refused because they were already married, but when they were threatened with death, they agreed to convert. "We were made to recite some words in Arabic and showed how to pray," the woman explained. "Then they let us go after three days because my mother promised we will convince our husbands to become Muslims."

Whatever the reason for each kidnapping, it is clear that teenagers, particularly girls, are a population at risk. Furthermore, non-Muslims are also targeted disproportionately. HRW interviewed thirty kidnapping victims who had been held in Boko Haram camps in the

Sambisa Forest Reserve and around the Gwoza hills. All but one were Christian. Their offenses seemed to be not being Muslim and attending secular school.

A Closer Look at Chibok

The kidnapping of more than two hundred high school students from the town of Chibok made international headlines, but it was not the first time Boko Haram had abducted a group of students. In February 2014, militants took twenty Government Girls Science College students. The Chibok kidnapping, about two months later, shone a light on the growing concern about Boko Haram abductions.

Late at night on April 14, 2014, a dorm full of sixteen-, seventeen-, and eighteen-year-old girls were preparing for the next day's tests. They were in the middle of the monthlong West African School Certificate examinations. Their schools had been shut down three weeks earlier because of Boko Haram, but the important tests were proceeding as planned. Suddenly, gunshots broke the silence. The teens ran to the windows and saw men arriving on motorcycles, shooting guns into the air.

According to a diary that students Naomi Adamu and Sarah Samuel kept together, with occasional input from some other friends, the Boko Haram militants intended to steal construction machinery from the school. What they found instead was a school full of teenage girls. "They started argument in their midst" about what to do with the girls, Adamu and Samuel wrote.

The young women scribbled their entries in the workbooks Boko Haram later gave them for their Quran studies. They wrote in English and Hausa, and the BBC shared excerpts after Adamu was released from Boko Haram in May 2017. Samuel agreed to marry one of the militants and, as of October 2017, remained missing.

Regarding the argument among the Boko Haram members the night of the Chibok kidnapping, some of the militants wanted to kill the girls, Adamu wrote. Some wanted to return them to their parents. Finally, one of them said, "'No, I can't come with empty car and go back with empty car … If we take them to Shekau, he will know what to do.'"

The men forced as many students as would fit into the one truck they had brought; the others marched at gunpoint for about 10 miles (16 km) to where the militants had more trucks. Three girls simply would not fit and were released. Over the first part of the journey, several others successfully escaped. They jumped from the backs of the moving trucks or, when the trucks stopped to replenish supplies, asked to go to the bathroom and then ran. Joy Bishara was one of those girls. She told the United Nations in 2017 that she threw herself from the truck and then ran for hours. She said she knew even then, so early in the ordeal, that she would rather be a "corpse in the ditch" than stay with Boko Haram.

The reason more girls did not jump was that, after the first few did, one of the girls reported the plan to the kidnappers. The BBC guessed that the girl disclosed the plan for any number of reasons, including being scared or being so used to respecting authority, as a young student, that she felt she needed to obey even her kidnappers.

The convoy continued to a camp deep in the forest. Two and a half years later, when some of the students were finally freed, the world learned what happened in the forest. In October 2016, twenty-one of the Chibok students were released after successful negotiations between Boko Haram and the Nigerian government. The *New York Times* reported what the young women said of their more than two years as hostages.

As soon as they arrived at Boko Haram's camp, the group of 219 students was given a choice by the terrorists: become wives for the soldiers or become their slaves. About half chose marriage. The released group of twenty-one did not come from that group. They came from the hundred or so who were forced into washing, fetching water, cooking, and meeting all other demands by the terrorists. Their food supply dwindled over the years, from rice and corn when they arrived to almost nothing by the time they left. The freed girls reported that some of their classmates died of starvation.

Jobs Around Camp

It is often assumed that kidnapped young women and girls are forced to cook and clean, acting as general maids around Boko Haram camps. That is sometimes the case, but they are just as often forced into other types of labor.

A fifteen-year-old said they were regularly ordered to carry back to camp what the insurgents stole from villages they had attacked. One nineteen-year-old described being made to trick members of the Civilian Joint Task Force (Civilian JTF), themselves teenagers, into following her. The Boko Haram soldiers then attacked the boys and killed them. They ordered the nineteen-year-old girl to kill the last one. When she refused, the camp leader's wife did it. Some of the youths' accounts are especially terrifying because they describe young women modeling destructive actions for other females or wishing work on others to lighten their own load. There were no allies in camp.

Even the cleaning was heavy with emotional impact. Girls and young women did not clean up just dirt but also blood.

Forced Marriages

Forced marriages between kidnapped teens and Boko Haram soldiers are common. Girls as young as nine become militants' wives. Sometimes the girls had no time to construct a plan to avoid marriage because they were given no notice about an impending wedding. Several girls reported that a fighter merely said a few words and then declared that the girl in front of him was now his wife.

Trying to Escape

For hostages of Boko Haram, the nightmare doesn't end even if they escape or are freed from their captors. Sometimes they have as much to fear from the neighbors they return to as they do from their ex-captors. "They're not trusted" by the community, Kimairis Toogood, a senior peacebuilding adviser with International Alert in Nigeria, told PBS *NewsHour*. Even though they did not choose to live with Boko Haram, they are guilty by association. Their communities feel they cannot trust the ex-hostages. They may have been brainwashed and could pose a threat. If they married a soldier or became pregnant while kidnapped, they were considered unclean. It did not matter that they had not chosen that life.

Communities also fear Boko Haram so much that they do not want to help people who escape from the group.

Many of the Chibok girls stayed on alert, desperate to find a time to escape the Boko Haram camp. At least one early attempt was ruined by the very people the girls hoped were on their side. Civilians in nearby towns were so scared of Boko Haram's retaliation if they helped the escaped girls that they returned them to their captors. Adamu and Samuel wrote that the girls "entered into a shop and asked [the people there] to help them and give them water and biscuit. So, the people asked them, 'Who are you and where did you come from?' The girls said, 'We are those that the BH [Boko Haram] kidnapped from GGSS [Government Girls Secondary School], Chibok.' So, one of the people said, 'Are these not Shekau's children?' So they gave them good food to eat and a place to sleep and the next day, they returned them to our place."

Even if ex-hostages successfully rejoin their communities, they themselves may remain Boko Haram targets. According to HRW, Boko Haram sought revenge against a nineteen-year-old, not from the Chibok group, after she escaped them. Members of the terrorist organization disguised themselves as Civilian JTF and reported the nineteen-year-old's brother to the police. He was arrested for suspicion of being a member of Boko Haram. After two weeks, the police arrested him. Then Boko Haram set fire to the escaped woman's home and all four churches in her village. Her entire family was displaced. "Even now I am still afraid," she told HRW.

Returning Home

The Nigerian government has said it is wary about conducting rescue operations out of fear of putting hostages at risk. Those at the scene of the rescue could get accidentally shot. Those held elsewhere could be used as pawns—their Boko Haram captors could hurt them in retaliation for the government's rescue attempt elsewhere. It has also been difficult to even locate hostages. It is suspected that Boko Haram hides its hostages whenever they hear surveillance aircraft approaching. Despite this, there have been some successes.

On May 17, 2016, over two years since her abduction from her school in Chibok, Amina Ali Nkeki came home. She had been nineteen years old at the time of her disappearance. Two years as a captive of a hostage organization had aged her beyond her twenty-one years, but she was still recognizable. Aboku Gaji, a member of the Civilian JTF, was patrolling the edge of the Sambisa Forest when he saw a dirty-looking woman and a man with a baby emerge from the trees. Immediately, he wondered if she was one of the Chibok students.

Gaji helped them into town. He later told BBC that Nkeki's mother was overjoyed to see her daughter. "She gave her the biggest hug ever, as if they were going to roll on the ground, we had to stabilize them," he said. Authorities questioned the two. They learned the four-month-old baby, Safiya, was Nkeki's, conceived and born while Nkeki was a hostage. The man was Mohammed Hayatu, whom both claimed was Nkeki's husband. This was where the story got confusing. Nkeki and Hayatu said they both were kidnapping victims of Boko Haram. Though they had both been forced into the marriage, they now loved each other. The Nigerian government said Hayatu was a Boko Haram terrorist, and they took him away for interrogation.

Since then, other Chibok girls have returned home, most released from captivity after negotiations between authorities and the terrorists. As of early 2018, the largest release of girls was a group of eighty-two in May 2017.

Months of negotiations in both Switzerland and Sudan preceded the release. Five imprisoned Boko Haram commanders were freed in exchange for the students' freedom. Nigerian senator Shehu Sani told the *Guardian* that he "came up with a road map for the talks." He introduced the Nigerian government and the lawyer who served as chief negotiator. At the time, the lawyer ran an orphanage in northeast Nigeria, the region most affected by Boko Haram. Previously, he was the personal attorney for Mohammed Yusuf, the founder of Boko Haram. The

International Committee of the Red Cross (ICRC) acted as a "neutral intermediary."

Experts did not worry that the released terrorists would strengthen Boko Haram as an organization. "Commanders could have a localized impact in areas that they return to," one analyst told the *Guardian*, "but it will have no wider impact." Experts did express concern about how the freed girls would be treated. Amnesty International's country director for Nigeria said that the former prisoners did not "deserve to be put through a publicity stunt … The government should respect their privacy and ensure that the released girls are reunited with their families and not kept in lengthy detention and security screening which can only add to their suffering and plight."

Amnesty International was likely basing its concern on what happened with the twenty-one Chibok students who were released seven months before, in October 2016. As of May 2017, those girls were still being held by the government, five hundred miles from their families. The government claimed they were receiving counseling, but they needed to also be reintegrated with their communities.

In January 2018, the Nigerian military said it rescued one more Chibok student. Salomi Pogu had escaped Boko Haram's camp and was surviving in the wilderness. A spokesperson for the town of Chibok agreed the person found was likely Pogu, the student, but he had yet to confirm with her parents. After Pogu was kidnapped, her parents had been threatened by Boko Haram and had fled to a camp for IDPs, and there was no phone access there.

Less than two weeks later, Boko Haram released a twenty-one-minute video showing about twelve to fourteen teenagers and young women. Some held babies. The group said these were Chibok students remaining in captivity, though neither Reuters nor Al Jazeera, reporting on the video, could verify the identities of the young people. In the video, the girls said they did not want to return home, claiming, "These people are taking care of us and we are grateful to them. We are happy here—we have found our faith." It was impossible to tell if the girls had been forced to say this, or if they truly believed it. Experts were doubtful that the video is anything but Boko Haram propaganda. This is based on information from freed girls, who said they were not treated well by the militants. Also, Nigerian President Muhammadu Buhari's New Year's message just days before the video said that he considered Boko Haram almost defeated. An Al Jazeera correspondent said analysts believe the video was released "to give Boko Haram an advantage in negotiations" and "to show that Boko Haram is still a potent force." This book's final chapter, next, explores some ways that Nigerians, and people everywhere, can help weaken Boko Haram, so that the frequency of their violence lessens.

Two young men attend a parade in Lagos in 2017. Young people can help efforts to put an end to Boko Haram.

CHAPTER FIVE

SOLVING TERROR

For its 2016 report on Boko Haram and teens, Mercy Corps researchers did not talk only to young people who had joined the terrorist organization. They also interviewed twenty-six young people who had resisted the militants' recruitment methods. Sixteen were males, and ten were females. Their backgrounds were as diverse as those of the youth who became members of Boko Haram. They had different education levels and worked in different fields. Understanding why they were able to resist can help experts understand where to allocate resources.

The Importance of Community

The more interpersonal connections a young person has, the less likely he or she is to get involved with Boko Haram. This is because they care about their friends and family and want to stay with them. They do not feel desperate to make connections elsewhere. They also then have access to people who remind them that Boko Haram does bad things, and people who will support them to improve society and push Boko Haram out of their communities. These activities echo two of Mercy Corps' recommendations that encourage communities and government to work together and support families, mentorships, and role models.

Conversations and Social Groups

Youth believe trusted adults when they talk openly about the corruption and violence of Boko Haram. "Our elders have also been warning us to be careful with them as they are deceiving," one young man from Borno told Mercy Corps. Conversations with parents also helped. A young woman from Gombe told Mercy Corps, "My father always talked to us about the negative impact of the sect and essence of Western education. We used to discuss and debate with [family members] and they know I will not join them."

Young people who had resisted joining Boko Haram explained why they did so by using words that echoed how village elders spoke. This indicated that what the elders said mattered. A Borno leader told Mercy Corps researchers that he counseled youth about the connection between economics and violence in Boko Haram. He told them that the leaders would make money off the young people's work and would never suffer consequences, while the young recruits would become poor and eventually be killed. A teen confirmed he heard this talk from adults by telling Mercy Corps researchers that he noticed how Boko Haram leaders kept getting richer while communities continued to grow poorer. One male youth from Borno told Mercy Corps, "All I know is that the leaders were always collecting money from the followers and while they were living in luxury, they made sure that all the followers were living in poverty."

Another Borno leader said that he preached that religion is used as a "strategy" by Boko Haram. Some young people told Mercy Corps that they saw through Boko Haram's religious claims. It seemed they connected with their community leaders' regular speeches on this topic. Mercy Corps researchers found that more than half of the youth who resisted joining Boko Haram said they saw the group as filled with corruption. They understood that its leaders were merely trying to make money.

It also helped when young people had strong social connections with peers, including with people in other communities. One young man told Mercy Corps that as the head of a youth group, he was of interest to Boko Haram. The very social network the terrorists wanted him to exploit on their behalf actually helped the young man to resist joining Boko Haram. His friends rallied around him and encouraged him to stay with them. Another young person told the researchers that he appreciated all his friends, so he was not attracted to the social isolation Boko Haram demanded. For many, keeping established friendships was more important than any personal gain that Boko Haram promised. If they had friends or relatives in other villages, they knew they had a wide safety net if Boko Haram attacked their village. They could turn to help elsewhere.

Direct Action

Adder Abel Gwoda, cofounder of the nongovernmental organization African Positive Peace Initiative and founder of the youth movement Youth Dynamics for the Development and Emergence of Cameroon, is working on a deradicalization process for young people, at the request of a Cameroonian army general. That is an important detail, that a representative of the state military wants to support positive community action. Instead of talking about Boko Haram (a negative topic), Gwoda is focusing on social assistance (a positive subject). His group offers schooling resources, food and farm resources, and health screenings to communities that are vulnerable to Boko Haram's influences.

Other advocates, like Achaleke Christian, founder of Local Youth Corner Cameroon, agree that it is more useful to focus on what can be done, not what is wrong. "Agents of radicalization craft messages around grievances, government failure, and religion to get youths involved," he told the IRIN news service. "We are sending out messages that violence is not the solution to these problems … We are also [urging] the government to play its role by eradicating the drivers of radicalization."

Toumba Haman was eighteen years old when Boko Haram attacked his hometown of Amchide, Cameroon. He watched friends join the terrorist organization even after the group had killed thirty of their neighbors and set fire to homes and businesses. "They were easily convinced because they were uneducated and poor," Haman told IRIN.

Three years later, in 2017, Haman has found success by staying in school. He and his college friends have founded an organization to encourage others to do the same. "We want to go back and encourage our peers to go to school," Haman said. "I feel like I owe my community."

Other young people feel like they owe their community through other types of action. Young men, most between the ages of fifteen and thirty-five, have formed the Civilian Joint Task Force (Civilian JTF), named after Nigeria's official Joint Military Task Force. These are everyday youth—carrying AK-47s, axes, knives, and bows and arrows. It may sound scary, but so far at least, they haven't provided a bad alternative. "Everyone trusts the Civilian JTF more than the military," Agafi Kunduli told the *Daily Beast*. He was a thirty-three-year-old program developer for a nongovernmental organization who spent his nights volunteering to guard his neighborhood. "Staying up late, it's worth it," he said. "Your brothers and sisters can go out in the morning and come back safely [and] the school cannot be bombed." The Civilian JTF even has undercover agents. They secretly gather information about Boko Haram and give it to the state military.

In 2013, the Borno state government officially acknowledged their community members' work. About two thousand Civilian JTF members received some free military training. The government gave the group uniforms and even promised to pay the twenty-six thousand registered members about $100 a month. However, according to a 2016 article posted on the Voice of America News website, the pay hasn't come.

THE NIGERIAN LITERARY RESURGENCE

Despite facing newsmaking issues like those created by Boko Haram, Nigeria also shines with greatness in the literary world. In fact, it is in part because of controversial subjects like the rise of Boko Haram, as well as general violence against women, that young Nigerian authors are experimenting and audiences are interested in their creations.

Nigerian writers of the past—like Chinua Achebe, who wrote *Things Fall Apart*, a novel that became required reading in many schools around the world, and Wole Soyinka, who was the first African to win the Nobel Prize for Literature—often found fame first outside of their home country. Authors today are finding and carving out a different reality. "There are more avenues for Nigerian writers to express themselves now, and people are being more bold," Abubakar Adam Ibrahim says. Born in 1979, he is considered part of the new generation of Nigerian authors.

He publishes with Cassava Republic Press, which was founded in 2006 but started releasing its books in the United States in 2017. It built its foundation with Nigerian writers and readers before expanding to the world. The press did this deliberately. "One of the things we are trying to do is expand the definition of African literature," says Bibi Bakare-Yusuf, Cassava Republic's cofounder and publisher.

That makes community leaders nervous. If the government will not or cannot follow through on that promise, what is their true opinion of, and perspective about, the Civilian JTF? Community leaders wonder if the government understands not only how much the young group has done but also how well armed they are. "They now know how to handle arms and ammunitions. They are trained in the art of warfare. If after the insurgency you abandon them, then you are planting another seed of discord," one leader told Voice of America News. "They have sacrificed their lives. That's why we've been arguing with the government to make sure that something is quickly put in place before the end of the insurgency."

There has been some positive response from the government. In 2015, the state security service gave about thirty Civilian JTF members permanent work. The next year, 350 Civilian JTF members joined the Nigerian army. All of these young men went through the proper recruitment and application process. Community leaders hope the government will be willing to help all members, even those who don't want a job or aren't qualified for government work. The government could give plots of land, one leader suggested as an example. That would be a nice reward for all Civilian JTF members, even those who want to start or maintain careers outside the military. "I'm a student, and I know what I'm doing in my life," Haruna Issa, a Civilian JTF member, told Voice of America News. He wanted to continue his college computer science courses.

Building Trust in the Government

Mercy Corps' report also recommended that Nigerian officials focus on building community trust in the government in order to eliminate Boko Haram. Boko Haram has survived in part because Nigerians are frustrated by a government that has for too long been seen as corrupt and untrustworthy. People want leaders who will improve society and help individual lives. If they could trust elected officials, they may not be so willing to believe Boko Haram.

This is a tall order, and not just because the government has to work hard to reverse its decades of mismanagement. Even its attempts to get rid of Boko Haram can end up hurting civilians. The Nigerian military will sometimes set fire to towns to force Boko Haram soldiers to flee. The side effect is, of course, that innocent civilians lose their homes and businesses, and sometimes their lives.

UNICEF told the story of Fati, who was thirteen when she was forced at gunpoint to join Boko Haram. A child bride of an adult soldier, she was considered as much an enemy of the state as any other Boko Haram member. UNICEF wrote that Fati was constantly on the move, targeted by Nigerian and Cameroonian soldiers and fighter jets. "Those jets, they bombed everybody, not only Boko Haram," she told UNICEF. In 2017, Isa Sanusi, media manager for Amnesty International Nigeria, echoed Fati's concerns in an interview with *Teen Vogue*.

Positive Steps

However, Sanusi felt that, overall, the government was doing the best it could. For example, in 2015, a coalition of the militaries of Nigeria, Chad, Cameroon, and Niger contained Boko Haram in the Sambisa Forest, greatly reducing the group's territory. When asked how successful the Nigerian military has been in combating Boko Haram and other extremist groups, Sanusi pointed to the Nigerian government's ability to stop Boko Haram from launching missiles and the government's reclamation of territory from the terrorist group.

Muhammadu Buhari, president since 2015, has asked the international community to return the billions of dollars embezzled from Nigeria and hidden in other countries' financial systems. He has been the only president to publicly demand that other countries acknowledge their complicity and correct the issue.

Furthermore, by 2016, the Nigerian government had a new strategy for rebuilding the areas destroyed by Boko Haram. The new Office of the Vice President and the President's Committee for the Northeast Initiative (PCNI) could "rebuild trust with communities by effectively implementing community-driven recovery and development initiatives." The program will succeed only if national leaders listen to what communities, including their young people, say they need. National and international support of local service groups and religious and media organizations will actually spread messages.

How to Help

One of the most important ways that teens outside of Nigeria can help those affected every day by Boko Haram is to keep talking about the situation. Young people in the United States and Canada have access to social media, which can carry a message far and wide. Also, their government officials have the responsibility to listen to their constituents—which teens are, too, even if they are not old enough to vote.

When the teenagers in Chibok, Nigeria, were abducted, the world reacted. The hashtag #BringBackOurGirls was used in a million tweets even before then–First Lady Michelle Obama herself used it. After her tweet, word spread exponentially. Years later, many of the Chibok students remain hostages. Those who have been freed are now experiencing the long, hard process of reentering their normal lives. Yet that hashtag, and other media coverage, is not as strong as it used to be. You can start reminding people of the story and post any developing news, hashtagging everything with #BringBackOurGirls.

In 2017, *Teen Vogue* asked Isa Sanusi, media manager for Amnesty International Nigeria, about the effect of #BringBackOurGirls. Sanusi said hashtag activism—or talking about an issue online and making sure others see it by labeling it—does help. Sanusi listed four reasons why it is important. One, she said, is that "hashtag activism in the case of Boko Haram opens the door to more direct and effective communication between Nigerians and their government, as well as the rest of the world." Properly labeled, or hashtagged, messages and posts help organize a worldwide discussion on a topic. People from presidents through elementary school students can talk with each other and read what others are saying. Two, Sanusi said, hashtag activism "tells Nigerians that they can use the power and reach of social media to demand change and compel government to take action on issues of general public interest." Not everyone grew up with the internet always within reach, and not everyone is used to knowing their opinions matter. By demonstrating the power of talking on social media, teens in the West can embolden teens in Nigeria. Three, Sanusi continued, "the hashtag helped a lot in making Nigerian authorities do more in taming the activities of Boko Haram in northeast Nigeria." If a topic is popular, authorities know that the world is watching them deal with it. Four, all the talk about Nigeria, "helped put pressure on the government to focus on ensuring accountability, making sure that all the girls abducted by Boko Haram are safely rescued and reunited with their families." Not only does hashtag activism encourage governments to act, but it encourages them to keep the public updated on how they're acting.

This is the case everywhere. It's important to hold other governments accountable for their response to Nigeria and Boko Haram too. Learn what your country is doing abroad and why. Call and email your government leaders about what decisions of theirs you like and what concerns you. Expressing your opinion really can lead to change.

OJONWA MIACHI

Two young people use their smartphones in Lagos. Staying connected online helps activists make a difference.

Thanks to Ojonwa Miachi's strong-willed parents, she got an education that has encouraged her, in turn, to fight for the rights of other Nigerian girls and women. Her parents had five children, all girls. Their neighbors in Nigeria encouraged them not to spend their money on school for them because they were "just girls" and therefore seen as not worth of a formal education. Miachi's parents disagreed.

Miachi ended up earning a degree in economics from Nigeria's Bingham University. At age twenty-one, in 2014, Miachi became a Global Youth Ambassador for A World at School. This organization encourages online youth activism around the globe. Miachi championed her organization's role in #BringBackOurGirls.

Miachi told media platform Devex, "I believe that the Nigerian government will give an ear to such views as may be expressed on social media … The reach of these petitions has been amazing and positive results have come forth." She also called the situation a "test case that should not be ignored." If Nigeria did not increase security and encourage girls to return to school, there would be long-term problems there and elsewhere in the world.

CHRONOLOGY

800 BCE

The Nok people settle what is now Nigeria.

1472   Europeans arrive on the shores of Nigeria.

1914   The British determine the modern-day borders of Nigeria.

1960   Nigeria wins independence.

1967–1970

Nigeria experiences civil war.

2002   Inspired by Wahhabism, Muhammed Yusuf founds Boko Haram to overthrow Nigeria's secular government and replace it with an Islamic one.

2009   The Nigerian government and Boko Haram engage in their first major battle, and Yusuf is killed; Abubakar Shekau becomes leader of Boko Haram.

2014   Boko Haram kidnaps more than two hundred students in Chibok, Nigeria.

2015   Boko Haram pledges its allegiance to ISIS.

2017   The terrorists of Boko Haram greatly increase their use of young suicide bombers.

GLOSSARY

census Official count or survey of a population.

Civilian Joint Task Force (Civilian JTF) Civilians who are fighting Boko Haram.

Convention on the Rights of the Child An international treaty outlining human rights—including civil, political, economic, social, health, and cultural—for children.

coup The forcible removal of a country's leadership from power.

detonate To cause to explode.

displacement Moving someone to a new location, usually because of instability or violence.

front line The part of an armed force that is closest to the enemy.

hashtag activism Talking about an issue online and making sure others see it by labeling it with a common phrase others are also using.

indirect rule A system where one government rules another nation, though the governed people retain certain administrative, legal, and other powers.

insurgent A person who forcibly opposes the authority lawfully in place.

internally displaced person (IDP) A person who is forced to flee from home but remains within his or her country, as opposed to a refugee, who goes to another country.

International Criminal Court (ICC) First permanent court investigating and trying cases on a global level.

ISIS The Islamic State of Iraq and Syria, a terrorist organization.

jihad Fights against the so-called enemies of Islam.

nonstate military An organized military that is not a country's official military.

Optional Protocol on the Involvement of Children in Armed Conflict (OPAC) First treaty to focus on ending military exploitation of people under age eighteen throughout the world. People charged with using youth as soldiers can be taken to court.

Oyinbo Someone who is not Nigerian.

propaganda Biased information used to promote a particular point of view.

recovery The removal of child soldiers from their armed forces.

recruitment The act of convincing someone to join armed forces.

reintegration The process through which ex–child soldiers return to civilian life.

relative deprivation The gap between what people think they deserve, based on what they see others have, and what they expect to get.

sharia law Islamic law.

suicide bomber Someone who carries explosives; children who do this are manipulated or forced to do so.

Tsangaya schools A traditional Islamic school system.

United Nations High Commissioner for Refugees (UNHCR) A program to protect and assist refugees and forcibly displaced people.

Wahhabism A form of Islam, dominant in Saudi Arabia.

FURTHER INFORMATION

Books

Lin, Yong Jui, and Patricia Levy. *Cultures of the World: Nigeria*. New York: Cavendish Square, 2014.

Okeowo, Alexis. *A Moonless, Starless Sky: Ordinary Women and Men Fighting Extremism in Africa.* New York: Hachette Books, 2017.

Thurston, Alexander. Boko Haram: *The History of an African Jihadist Movement*. Princeton, NJ: Princeton University Press, 2017.

Websites

CIA World Factbook: Nigeria

https://www.cia.gov/library/publications/
the-world-factbook/geos/print_ni.html

Find maps, statistics, and information Nigeria's history on this website created by the CIA.

Mapping Militant Organizations: Boko Haram

http://web.stanford.edu/group/mappingmilitants/
cgi-bin/groups/view/553?highlight=boko+haram

Stanford University provides a history of Boko Haram as well as maps that show how Boko Haram works with terrorist groups like ISIS and al-Qaeda.

Videos

"My Nigeria"

http://www.aljazeera.com/programmes/my-nigeria/
Al Jazeera produced six films on everyday life in Nigeria.

"On Humanity"

https://www.ted.com/talks/chris_abani_muses_on_humanity

Chris Abani gives a TED Talk on being
human and reclaiming humanity.

BIBLIOGRAPHY

Adamczyk, Ed. "Boko Haram Recruited 2,000 Child Soldiers in 2016: UNICEF." UPI, February 21, 2017. https://www.upi.com/Top_News/World-News/2017/02/21/Boko-Haram-recruited-2000-child-soldiers-in-2016-UNICEF/8831487689926/.

Agence France-Presse. "Tour Reveals Shady Nigerian Cash behind London Luxury Homes." News24, October 6, 2017. https://www.news24.com/Africa/News/tour-reveals-shady-nigerian-cash-behind-london-luxury-homes-20171006.

Ahmed, Sana. "In Their Own Words: Ojonwa Miachi." Global Business Coalition for Education, September 11, 2015. http://gbc-education.org/in-their-own-words-ojonwa-miachi/.

Alter, Alexandra. "A Wave of New Fiction from Nigeria, as Young Writers Experiment with New Genres." New York Times, November 23, 2017. https://www.nytimes.com/2017/11/23/books/fiction-nigeria-writers.html.

Barrett, A. Igoni. "I Remember the Day ... I Designed the Nigerian Flag." Al Jazeera, September 3, 2015. http://www.aljazeera.com/programmes/my-nigeria/2015/09/nigerian-flag-150901092231928.html.

Bavier, Joe. "Who Are Boko Haram and Why Are They Terrorizing Nigerian Christians?" *Atlantic*, January 24, 2012. https://www.theatlantic.com/international/archive/2012/01/who-are-boko-haram-and-why-are-they-terrorizing-nigerian-christians/251729/.

BBC Monitoring. "Is Islamic State Shaping Boko Haram Media?" BBC, March 4, 2015. http://www.bbc.com/news/world-africa-31522469.

Busari, Stephanie, and Bryony Jones. "Escaped Chibok Girl: I Miss My Boko Haram Husband." CNN. August 17, 2016. http://www.cnn.com/2016/08/16/africa/chibok-girl-amina-ali-nkeki-boko-haram-husband/.

Busari, Stephanie, and Tim Hume. "First Missing Chibok Girl Found after 2 Years as Boko Haram Prisoner." CNN, May 18, 2016. http://edition.cnn.com/2016/05/18/africa/nigeria-chibok-girl-found/index.html.

"Chibok Diaries: Chronicling a Boko Haram Kidnapping." BBC, October 23, 2017. http://www.bbc.com/news/world-africa-41570252.

Cooper, Helene. "Boko Haram and ISIS Are Collaborating More, U.S. Military Says." *New York Times*, April 20, 2016. https://www.nytimes.com/2016/04/21/world/africa/boko-haram-and-isis-are-collaborating-more-us-military-says.html.

Diamond, Jeremy. "France and Nigeria: 2 Countries Rocked by Terror with Very Different Reactions." CNN, January 13, 2015. https://www.cnn.com/2015/01/13/politics/paris-nigeria-attacks-comparison/index.html.

Epatko, Larisa. "Surviving Boko Haram: Kidnapped Girls Tell Their Stories." PBS *Newshour,* October 19, 2016. http://www.pbs.org/newshour/updates/surviving-boko-haram-kidnapped-girls-tell-stories/.

Gaffey, Conor. "Buhari to the World: Hurry Up and Return Nigeria's Stolen Money." *Newsweek*, May 6, 2016. http://www.newsweek.com/nigerias-buhari-tells-world-hurry-and-return-our-stolen-money-456467.

Gidda, Mirren. "Boko Haram Is Growing Stronger in Nigeria Thanks to Corruption in the Military." *Newsweek*, May 19, 2017. http://www.newsweek.com/nigeria-defense-spending-corruption-boko-haram-611685.

Gilbert, Dami. "Exploring Education Differences: Life Inside a Nigerian School." ThreeSixty Journalism, March 7, 2013. http://threesixtyjournalism.org/nigerianschools.

Guilbert, Kieran. "Watch out Wonder Woman: Nigeria's Chibok girls inspire Marvel's new superhero." Reuters, September 6, 2017. https://www.reuters.com/article/us-nigeria-entertainment-chibok/watch-out-wonder-woman-nigerias-chibok-girls-inspire-marvels-new-superhero-idUSKCN1BH1HG.

Maclean, Ruth, Isaac Abrak, and others. "ISIS Tries to
Impose New Leader on Boko Haram in Nigeria."
Guardian, August 4, 2016. https://www.theguardian.com/
world/2016/aug/05/isis-tries-to-impose-new-leader-on-
boko-haram-in-nigeria.

Maclean, Ruth, and Alice Ross. "82 Chibok Schoolgirls Freed
in Exchange for Five Boko Haram Leaders." *Guardian*,
May 7, 2017. https://www.theguardian.com/world/2017/
may/07/chibok-schoolgirls-familes-await-as-82-are-
freed-by-boko-haram-exchange-prison.

Mark, Monica. "Yola: The City Where People Fleeing Boko
Haram Outnumber 400,000 Locals." *Guardian*, January
28, 2015. https://www.theguardian.com/world/2015/
jan/28/boko-haram-nigeria-yola-refugees-monica-mark-
adamawa.

Mercy Corps. *"Motivations and Empty Promises": Voices of
Former Boko Haram Combatants and Nigerian Youth.*
April 2016. https://www.mercycorps.org/sites/default/
files/Motivations%20and%20Empty%20Promises_
Mercy%20Corps_Full%20Report.pdf.

Moore, Jack. "Twitter Shuts Down Boko Haram Account."
Newsweek, February 25, 2015. http://www.newsweek.
com/twitter-shuts-down-boko-haram-account-309320.

Nakell, Patricia. "Fati Was Kidnapped by Boko Haram. This Is Her Story." UNICEF Australia, May 13, 2016. https://www.unicef.org.au/blog/stories/april-2016/kidnapped-by-boko-haram.

Neff, Zama. "Girls Kidnapped by Boko Haram Share Their Stories at UN." Human Rights Watch, October 16, 2017. https://www.hrw.org/news/2017/10/16/girls-kidnapped-boko-haram-share-their-stories-un.

Nwaubani, Adaobi Tricia. "A Day in the Life of … a House Girl." *Al Jazeera*, September 8, 2015. http://www.aljazeera.com/programmes/my-nigeria/2015/09/nigeria-life-house-girl-150906134841694.html.

Obaji Jr., Philip. "Why Boko Haram Keeps Bombing Nigeria's Mosques." *Daily Beast*, July 20, 2015. https://www.thedailybeast.com/why-boko-haram-keeps-bombing-nigerias-mosques.

Ocampo, Aimee Rae. "'A Test Case that Should Not Be Ignored.'" Devex, May 6, 2014. https://www.devex.com/news/a-test-case-that-should-not-be-ignored-83431.

Ochonu, Moses. "The Roots of Nigeria's Religious and Ethnic Conflict." Public Radio International, March 10, 2014. https://www.pri.org/stories/2014-03-10/roots-nigerias-religious-and-ethnic-conflict.

Oduah, Chika. "Nigeria Vigilantes Ponder Future After Fighting Boko Haram." Voice of America News, July 5, 2016. https://www.voanews.com/a/what-next-for-the-nigeria-vigilantes-fighting-boko-haram/3405851.html.

Raffey, Nick. "Operation Naberius: The Canadian Forces' Role in Combating Boko Haram." NAOC, March 25, 2017. http://natoassociation.ca/operation-naberius-the-canadian-forces-role-in-combating-boko-haram/.

Sadighi, Darius. "How Hashtag Activism Helped Raise Awareness About Boko Haram." *Teen Vogue*, May 12, 2017. https://www.teenvogue.com/story/hashtag-activism-raise-awareness-boko-haram.

Reuters. "Boko Haram 'Chibok Girls' Video a Propaganda Counter-strike, Say Analysts." Voice of America News, January 15, 2018. https://www.voanews.com/a/boko-haram-chibok-girls-video-a-propaganda-counterstrike-say-analysts/4209047.html.

Sahara Reporters. "Wife of Boko Haram Leader, Shekau, Killed in Military Strike." October 25, 2017. http://saharareporters.com/2017/10/25/wife-boko-haram-leader-shekau-killed-military-strike.

Searcey, Dionne. "Boko Haram Using More Children as Suicide Bombers, UNICEF Says." *New York Times*, April 12, 2016. https://www.nytimes.com/2016/04/13/world/africa/boko-haram-children-suicide-bombers-unicef-report.html.

Segun, Mausi, and Samer Muscati. *"'Those Terrible Weeks in Their Camp': Boko Haram Violence against Women and Girls in Northeast Nigeria."* Human Rights Watch, October 27, 2014. http://features.hrw.org/features/ HRW_2014_report/Those_Terrible_Weeks_in_Their_ Camp/assets/nigeria1014web.pdf.

Simpson, Gerry. "'They Forced Us onto Trucks Like Animals.'" Human Rights Watch, September 27, 2017. https://www.hrw.org/report/2017/09/27/they-forced-us- trucks-animals/cameroons-mass-forced-return-and- abuse-nigerian.

Sixtus, Mbom. "Young guns: Cameroon's Boko Haram problem." IRIN, August 11, 2017. https://www.irinnews. org/analysis/2017/08/11/young-guns-cameroon-s- boko-haram-problem.

smartygirl10. "A Day in the Life of a Student in Nigeria." SparkNotes/SparkLife, August 16, 2010. http:// community.sparknotes.com/2010/08/16/a-day-in-the- life-of-a-student-in-nigeria.

Stein, Chris, and Dionne Searcey. "Chibok Schoolgirls, Reuniting with Parents, Tell of Boko Haram Slavery." *New York Times*, October 16, 2016. https://www. nytimes.com/2016/10/17/world/africa/21-nigerian-girls- reuniting-with-parents-tell-of-boko-haram-slavery.html.

Strochlic, Nina. "Nigeria's Do-It-Yourself Boko Haram Busters." *Daily Beast*, May 16, 2014. http://www. thedailybeast.com/articles/2014/05/16/nigeria-s-do-it-yourself-boko-haram-busters.html.

Zenn, Jacob. "Electronic Jihad in Nigeria: How Boko Haram Is Using Social Media." *Terrorism Monitor* 15, no. 23 (2017). https://jamestown.org/program/electronic-jihad-nigeria-boko-haram-using-social-media/.

INDEX

ABOUT THE AUTHOR

Kristin Thiel lives in Portland, Oregon. Among numerous other books, she is the author of *True Teen Stories from Syria: Surviving Civil War*. Thiel has worked on many of the books in the So, You Want to Be A … series, which offers career guidance for kids and is published by Beyond Words, an imprint of Simon & Schuster. She was the lead writer on a report for her city about funding for high school dropout prevention. Thiel has judged YA book contests and managed before-school and afterschool literacy programs for AmeriCorps VISTA.